Quick Draw

Fairies and Princesses

KINGFISHER

How to use this book

1. Trace the grid opposite. You can use any size of paper as long as the grid proportions are the same as the one in this book. The grid squares will help you position your drawing and ensure the different stages are correctly scaled.

2. Use a light pencil line to draw. That way you can rub out the lines much more easily.

3. Copy the shapes in step one, then add the new shapes in step two and so on. As you add each step, your picture will begin to take shape.

4. When you have copied each step, rub out the extra lines from the earlier step – to eventually reveal the final shape (as shown in the final step).

5. Now colour in your finished picture.

As you become more confident, you may find that you don't need the grid squares any more. You may wish to add your own finishing touches to the illustrations, such as background plants, to create a scene.

Dancing fairy

Step 1

Step 2

Step 3

Step 4

Step 5

Step 6

Step 7

Step 8

Fairytale knight

Step 1

Step 2

Step 3

Step 4

Step 5

Step 6

Step 7

Step 8

Fairytale princess

Step 1

Step 2

Step 3

Step 4

Step 5

Step 6

Step 7

Step 8

Fairytale prince

Step 1

Step 2

Step 3

Step 4

Step 5

Step 6

Step 7

Step 8

Queen

Step 1

Step 2

Step 3

Step 4

Step 5

Step 6

Step 7

Step 8

King

Step 1

Step 2

Step 3

Step 4

Step 5

Step 6

Step 7

Step 8

Cinderella

Step 1

Step 2

Step 3

Step 4

Step 5

Step 6

Step 7

Step 8

Fairy godmother

Step 1

Step 2

Step 3

Step 4

Step 5

Step 6

Step 7

Step 8

Princess wearing a ballgown

Step 1

Step 2

Step 3

Step 4

Step 5

Step 6

Step 7

Step 8

Pixie

Step 1

Step 2

Step 3

Step 4

Step 5

Step 6

Step 7

Step 8

Mermaid princess

Step 1

Step 2

Step 3

Step 4

Step 5

Step 6

Step 7

Step 8

Baby fairy

Step 1

Step 2

Step 3

Step 4

Step 5

Step 6

Step 7

Step 8

Tooth fairy

Step 1

Step 2

Step 3

Step 4

Step 5

Step 6

Step 7

Step 8

Wild strawberry fairy

Step 1

Step 2

Step 3

Step 4

Step 5

Step 6

Step 7

Step 8

KINGFISHER

Kingfisher Publications Plc
New Penderel House
283–288 High Holborn
London WC1V 7HZ
www.kingfisherpub.com

First published by Kingfisher Plc 2007
10 9 8 7 6 5 4 3 2 1

TS/0707/PROSP/IGS/120WOF/C

ISBN 978 0 7534 1612 9

Produced for Kingfisher by The Peter Bull Art Studio

For Kingfisher:
Associate Creative Director: Mike Davis
Designers: Ray Bryant and Emy Manby
Senior production controller: Jessamy Oldfield
DTP Manager: Nicky Studdart

A CIP catalogue record for this book is available from
the British Library.

Printed in China